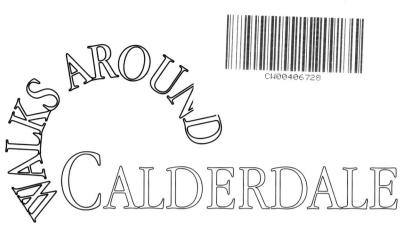

WALKS AROUND CALDERDALE

TEN WALKS OF SIX MILES OR UNDER

Dorian Speakman

Dalesman

First published in 2010 by Dalesman
an imprint of
Country Publications Ltd
The Water Mill
Broughton Hall
Skipton
North Yorkshire BD23 3AG

Text © Dorian Speakman 2010
Maps © Guelder Design & Mapping 2010
Illustrations © Christine Isherwood 2010

Cover: Hebden Bridge by Mike Kipling

ISBN 978-1-85568-271-9

Printed by Amadeus Press

PUBLISHER'S NOTE
....
The information given in this book has been provided in good faith and is intended only as a general guide. Whilst all reasonable efforts have been made to ensure that details were correct at the time of publication, the author and Country Publications Ltd cannot accept any responsibility for inaccuracies. It is the responsibility of individuals undertaking outdoor activities to approach the activity with caution and, especially if inexperienced, to do so under appropriate supervision. The activity described in this book is strenuous and individuals should ensure that they are suitably fit before embarking upon it. They should carry the appropriate equipment and maps, be properly clothed and have adequate footwear. They should also take note of weather conditions and forecasts, and leave notice of their intended route and estimated time of return.

Contents

Introduction

Calderdale is a dale of many features: from the high moorlands in the west to the heart of the West Yorkshire urban agglomeration in the east. On the way are hilltop villages perched on the shoulder of the dale and dramatically steep valley sides, often densely wooded with rushing streams and maybe a long lost mill by the waterside. The green pastures of the hills lie below the moors, the fields criss-crossed with drystone walls and paths, many of them ancient stone causeways. Down in the dale sit canal, railway and road, each providing a trans-Pennine link between the cities and towns of West Yorkshire and Lancashire.

Layers of history run through the dale, from the remains of ancient trading routes, and farmsteads dating back hundreds of years, to the beginnings of industrialisation. Mills appeared, first powered by water then coal, to be followed by reservoirs, railways and roads. More recent developments have been generated by renewable energy – from hilltop windfarms to single turbines in a back field.

The following ten walks are spread across the length of Calderdale. The first is in the lower reaches, at Mirfield, then the walks progress up the dale to finish in the western headwaters of the Calder, close to the Lancashire border. The first two walks are the easiest, taking fairly level routes. The others vary in terrain that is often hilly with steep sections. The final walk is the most demanding with a traverse of open moorland. The times given for the walks include an allowance for navigation, which at times needs care, be it over an expanse of moor or through a choice of lanes and tracks. Occasionally a grid reference is given for clarification.

All the walks are accessible throughout the year by public transport so, on a linear route, a return to a parked car is straightforward; details are supplied at the start of each walk. Train and bus times can be checked on the Metro website at www.wymetro.com.

Despite the proximity of towns in Calderdale, as you gain height temperature and exposure can change rapidly when you reach the open hillsides in contrast to the sheltered valleys so stout footwear and wind- and waterproof clothing are essential.

The author would like to thank Calderdale Council's Rights of Way Section for their helpful and efficient assistance.

Lower Calderdale

Length: 5 miles (8 km). Time: 3 hours.
Terrain: gentle gradient or level; climb of 130 feet (40m) nr Brighouse (can be avoided).
Start: Mirfield station.
Parking: Mirfield (parking by station limited at busy times)
Transport: trains from Leeds, Hebden Bridge, Halifax, Bradford, Huddersfield.
Finish: Brighouse station. Trains back to Mirfield. Trains to Hebden Bridge, Halifax, Huddersfield and Bradford. Frequent express buses for Bradford Interchange and Huddersfield.
Refreshments/facilities: pubs serving food at Mirfield, Colne Bridge and Brighouse. Toilets at Thornton Square, Brighouse.

Mirfield is not readily associated with Calderdale, lying as it does in Kirklees District, and on the Leeds to Huddersfield railway. However, the town is very much a part of the lower dale as this walk demonstrates. Taking in railway paths, canal towpaths, riverside paths and tracks, this route makes an interesting link along the valley and with the numerous transport routes that use it and cross it.

From the station, the platform exits lead down to the road running under the railway lines. Follow the road towards Mirfield town centre, turning left by the pub where a footpath is signed. The path leads off the left fork behind the pub down a passageway to emerge at the next road. Turn left here and cross over the road to go under the railway and over the river.

Take the next right following the blue Calder Valley cycleway signs to pass in front of the school and the cycle path ahead. The route now follows the cycleway as it parallels the railway passing over a filled-in bridge along the way. The cycle path ends by a road; continue along the Calder Valley cycleway by following the road in the same direction; traffic should be very light.

Fine views appear across the Calder Valley ahead. The copper roof of the Mirfield community church is a distinct landmark – the building and its grounds are now home to a monastic order.

Field vole: found in moist, grassy areas

5

After 500 yards, past the plantation on the right, the cycle path starts again, to lead through some trees and dip down before meeting the busy Bog Green Lane. Cross with care to continue on the cycle path, wide views across the valley appearing. Take the grassy footpath which crosses the cycleway, turning right to take a short but steep descent to the right of the terrace of houses. At the bottom turn right on the road to meet the main road again at Colne Bridge.

At Colne Bridge the River Colne meets the Calder, and it is here the railways, roads and canal from Huddersfield meet and join others.

Cross at the bridge and follow the road up to the Huddersfield Broad Canal; a footpath leading off to the right joins the canal. Turn right onto the towpath and follow it as it descends by the locks to go under the railway bridge. Shortly afterwards the canal bends round close to the River Calder to culminate in the No 1 lock meeting the River Calder.

Huddersfield Broad Canal connects Huddersfield with the rest of the canal network at the Calder and Hebble Navigation. Just 3¾ miles (6km) long, it was completed in 1780 by the Ramsden family of Huddersfield. A short distance (400 yards) down the main road is the Dumb Steeple, a meeting point for the Luddites before their attack and subsequent deadly battle at Cartwright Mill in Rawfolds in 1812.

Cross over the little footbridge and the take the path under the road bridge to cross the road safely. Turn back left to go up to the road and then pass the garage to take the next street right, Lower Quarry Road.

Follow the street along as it becomes a narrow lane, crossing over a railway; after the last row of terraces take the track forking right, which descends to cross the railway once again. The track winds round along the river terrace before bending left to cross under another railway bridge, and then the track goes across open fields. Eventually take the right turn at the T junction below the house to approach the canal bridge. Go left to go down the steps to join the Calder & Hebble Navigation canal, a short branch off the river Calder. Continue along the towpath as it heads towards the wooded hillside, passing under the high bridge carrying the M62 motorway.

The path leads towards some houses which meet the lock where the branch of the canal rejoins the river. Soon after the track bends right following the river but, instead, at a passing place on the left, take the footpath leading off. This path leads off behind the factory, and then at a perimeter fence bend left; then the path approaches the railway. After following close to the railway, the path bends right and finishes by a stone road bridge.

At this point the approach into Brighouse gives two options. The most direct is to follow the road by going straight ahead along the passageway and

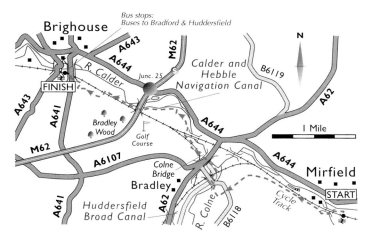

continuing for about ¾ mile (1km), until the station appears just before the main A62. This route is a bit of an anticlimax, passing through mainly industrial buildings and warehouses.

Alternatively, take the steps up the side of the bridge and follow the road over the railway up to the mini-roundabout. Take the right turn and then the next right. This road leads up through a residential area, climbing steadily before levelling off. After the street bends left, turn right onto Stratton Park.

A fine view of Brighouse appears and it is evident how the town has spread from the valley up the hillsides.

Almost immediately after, take the path leading off right down through the trees. Ignore the turn-off to continue descending, behind the terraced houses, to emerge at a road end. Follow the street as it passes the rows of terraces (the railway being walled off to the right) to its junction with the A62. Turn right to get to Brighouse station.

For Brighouse town centre, continue along the main road down the hill, straight ahead at the lights and over the river. On the left are the bus stops for the X6 or 393 to Bradford (the same buses for Huddersfield on the other side of Huddersfield Road).

The Salterhebble Canal

Length: 4¼ miles (6¾ km). **Time:** 2¼ - 2½ hours.
Terrain: gentle gradient or level, mostly on paved or tarmac surfaces.
Parking: Halifax town centre or Sowerby Bridge town centre
Start: Halifax railway station. Frequent trains to Leeds and Hebden Bridge,
Bradford, Manchester and Burnley. **Finish:** Sowerby Bridge town centre.
Frequent buses to Halifax. Half hourly trains to Hebden Bridge and Leeds.
Hourly service back to Halifax and Bradford.
Refreshments/facilities: plenty in Halifax town centre and Sowerby Bridge;
pubs at Boys Lane, Salterhebble Canal basin, Sowerby Bridge. Toilets at
Wharf Street, Sowerby Bridge.
Cut-off point: Salterhebble canal basin.

This walk starts in Halifax's industrial heart. Taking the Hebble Trail, the route threads its way though the industrial past of the town, down the Hebble Brook – site of works old and new. This section is enclosed by walls and some might not wish to walk it alone.

Lower down the valley the route is more wooded with a backdrop of fine old nineteenth century mill buildings before it joins the Salterhebble Canal which linked Halifax by water to the rest of the country. Following the canal we then enter Calderdale and the wooded environs of the valley floor with hints of the heavy industrial past lining the route which has been much improved in recent years. The finish in Sowerby Bridge, a small town on the edge of Halifax, provides a choice of pubs and eateries.

From Halifax station go through the approach road car park and turn right, following the paved path as the road bends off to the left. This shortly joins Church Street; follow this down to the roundabout. Take the right exit, which runs under the railway viaduct, and straight after take the enclosed path which is just to the right of the Nestlé factory entrance.

Where the path splits, take the path following the high wall, and continue until it ends and descends on a short cobbled section of road. Follow the road over the bridge past Hargreaves Foundry. At the road end there is a noticeboard about the Hebble Trail which links Halifax town centre with the Salterhebble Canal basin.

The Hebble Trail: much of the area you have just walked through has an interesting past dating from the sixteenth century, and the noticeboard gives

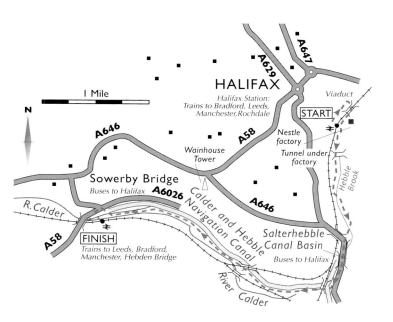

a detailed description of the industrial history including one disaster that befell a mill, when a whole floor collapsed causing many deaths.

Cross over the road taking the path opposite down the steps. This leads under a building in a tunnel by the brook, before emerging in a walled corridor. The path follows the brook as fine mill buildings appear on the right.

The path emerges by a road bridge. Turn right to cross the Hebble Brook. Next turn left down a cobbled lane to pass behind Shears Inn, leading up to a wider cobbled road. After about 150 yards take the path on the left which leads down to a gap in the wall to a bridge. Cross over the bridge and follow the narrow road as it winds between the converted mills. Ahead the entrance to the Hebble Trail cycleway now appears marked by a blue sign. The track is hard surfaced and continues to follow the Hebble Brook downstream.

At the new houses the route follows a cobbled lane before continuing straight ahead.

Just before the main road take the path right which leads under a subway to emerge directly at a canal basin at the end of the Hebble Trail.

Bus stops on Salter Hebble Hill (the main road) are about 50 yards in the direction away from Halifax if you wish to start or return from here. Go left up the steps to continue alongside the canal along a wide towpath.

Several barges with long term moorings are sited here. The Watermill pub overlooks the canal basin. From now on the route follows the canal to Sowerby Bridge and is level all the way.

After about half a mile the canal reaches the Salterhebble Locks. Cross the canal by the bridge and turn right to continue towards Sowerby Bridge.

At this point the main valley of Calderdale is entered, the leafy environs of the canal junction and locks surrounded by criss-crossing roads and railways linking Halifax and upper Calderdale with Huddersfield, Dewsbury and Wakefield.

The canal passes the village of Copley before passing under the large railway viaduct.The surroundings become verdant as woodland appears on the right, and semi-wild woodland appears on the river floodplain to the left, often on the site of old mills. On the right the unmistakable Wainhouse Tower appears on the hillside.

Wainhouse Tower was built in 1875 originally with the purpose of dispersing smoke from the Washer Lane dyeworks. The owner, John Wainhouse, had decided that the chimney, rising 253 feet (77m) in height, would be an object of beauty. Though it was never used for its intended purpose, the tower was not a folly – it was used as an observation post during the Second World War. Today, the tower can be visited and those who climb its 403 steps are rewarded with fine views across Calderdale.

The canal leads into the town of Sowerby Bridge and near the centre, where the canal splits, metal posts note the start of the Rochdale Canal. Continue on the towpath as it leads along the canal bearing left, passing the boatyard of Sowerby Bridge Wharf.

After the second lock the towpath leads up to Town Hall Road.

For buses back to Halifax turn left, and cross the road at the pelican crossing for the bus stop.

For the railway station turn left along Town Hall Road, looking out for a small sign for the station set against a blue background. (The sign is at the same level as the shop signs.) Go down the narrow cobbled passageway which continues down to a bridge over the river to the railway station.

Around Ripponden

Distance: 3 miles (5 km). Time: 2 hours.
Terrain: one climb of 325 feet (100m). Footpaths and tracks.
Transport: Ripponden 560/561/566 from Halifax and Sowerby Bridge, from Rochdale 528 (daily). On Sundays from Sowerby Bridge and Halifax, buses 532/3 run hourly in addition to the two-hourly 560.
Parking in Ripponden: Royd Lane, 2 hours only.
Refreshments/facilities: pubs, cafes and toilets (Halifax Road) in Ripponden.
Cut-off point: Kebroyd

This walk takes in the hillside village of Soyland Town over to the neighbouring valley below Mill Bank, before following the woods back down to the Ryburn Valley. An undulating track follows the route of the old railway back up the valley to the village of Ripponden.

Golden plover

From Ripponden village centre go up Royd Lane which leads up the hill from the main road, at the Sowerby Bridge side of the traffic lights. Opposite the second bus stop, take the footpath opposite, signed as the Calderdale Way. The path leads out of Ripponden along the hillside, passing through a narrow stile before meeting a lane by a row of houses.

Go up the enclosed lane and at the next junction go straight ahead, then left to follow the walled lane uphill which narrows to a path. Where the path meets the road, turn right to enter (some delusions of grandeur here!) Soyland Town. Pass the first group of houses and then just before the next group on the right, take the path signed with a Calderdale Way symbol. This path soon meets a track, where you turn right. Just past the bend take the next footpath left, signed the Calderdale Way.

At this point wide views across the next valley open out across Mill Bank and the scattered hamlets beyond.

The path crosses the hillside before descending steeply down to Clapgate Lane. At the track turn left to go to the road and then turn sharp right to continue downhill to the old watermill. Just before the bridge take the path right leading off initially along the side of the stream. The path then gently rises away from the stream, going deeper into the woods.

11

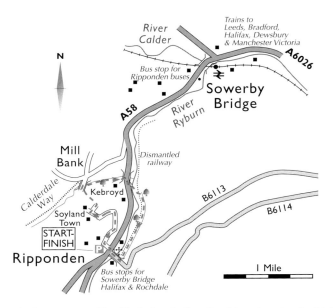

The path then passes old mills below before it widens to a track. At the sharp bend by the left wooden pole is a yellow waymark indicating the path which descends further. The path meets a drive which leads down the A58 main road at Kebroyd.

Turn right onto the road, and just after the bus stops take the track left which leads down to the River Ryburn. Take the bridge to cross over the river and follow the track up the slope, and then go over the old railway bridge. Turn right at the junction.

The old railway to Ripponden was originally intended as more than a branch line of the main Calder Valley. The route was envisaged as a main line into Lancashire, but, due to the high costs of engineering, only reached as far as Rishworth. Passenger trains on the line ceased in 1929.

Now follow the lane (Hangingstone Lane) for about ¾ mile (1km) as it parallels the dismantled railway. Eventually the lane joins a road; follow this to descend all the way to the church.

Go over the old humpbacked bridge passing the old Bridge Inn and up the steep cobbled road. The road emerges at the main road in the centre of Ripponden where the walk started. Buses to Sowerby Bridge and Halifax mostly leave from the main road on the opposite side (one uses Royd Lane), otherwise turn left for buses to Rochdale.

Ogden Water & Ovenden Moor

> **Distance: 3 miles (5km). Time: 1½ - 2 hours.**
> **Terrain: footpaths, some sections eroded.**
> **Start and finish: Ogden Water Visitor Centre.**
> **Transport: hourly buses 504 to Ogden from Halifax, Sundays 502 from Halifax and Keighley.**
> **Parking: Ogden Water car park, Ogden.**
> **Refreshments: Ogden Water Visitor Centre, pub at Causeway Foot, Ogden.**
> **Toilets at Ogden Water Visitor Centre.**

This walk takes in the moors above Ogden Water, easily reached from the high starting point of Ogden. There are fine views over Calderdale and Bradford District. Passing the wind farm of Ovenden Moor, the route drops down into a steep valley, through woodland and along the reservoir shore.

If travelling from Halifax on the bus, alight just past Halifax Golf Club entrance, before Ogden village. Past the Union Lane/Rock Lane junction, take the lane that peels off left where the main A629 bends right. Follow this track, marked 'Unsuitable for Motor Vehicles', up to Ogden Water.

Ogden Water is a 34-acre (14ha) reservoir surrounded by mixed woodland and is a designated Nature Reserve. Originally built by Halifax Water Corporation, the reservoir is now owned by Yorkshire Water and managed by Calderdale Council. The water and its surrounding woodland serve as an outdoor recreation area and educational centre. Located over 1,000 feet (300m) above sea level in the moors above Halifax, they also provide a rich contrast to the bleak open hillsides of peat and heather. The area is host to 130 species of birds.

From the car park of Ogden Water follow the road leading from the entrance down the slope to the reservoir, passing the Visitor Centre and toilets. Cross the reservoir along the dam wall and take the wide track that leads up the hill. The track climbs steadily, with the golf course on the left and the woods of Ogden Water on the right.

As you climb, excellent views of Halifax appear on the left and behind, and then over Calderdale itself; nearing the top the wind turbines of Ovenden Moor can be seen ahead.

After 1 mile (1.5km) the track begins to level out, turn right through a gate just before the track bends left towards the radio mast and houses, taking a

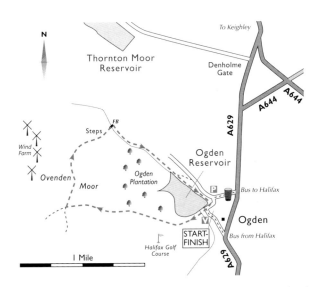

footpath which is a grassy track crossing the moor. Dominating the foreground is Ovenden Moor wind farm.

Ovenden Moor Wind Farm provides a spectacular sight on the hilltop – 23 wind turbines combine to produce up to 9.2 megawatts of electricity. Operating since 1993, the wind turbines are set out in a V formation, to make best use of the prevailing south-westerly winds. The turbines start operating at wind speeds of 11mph (17.5kph), but have to shut down for safety reasons when wind speeds exceed 56mph (90kph).

The track crosses a small bridge and gains a little more height, the surface getting increasingly eroded as you progress. Ahead are views over towards Airedale and, on the right, Bradford.

The track crosses the heather and begins to descend gradually before reaching a small gate. After the gate a deep ravine appears ahead, the path using stone steps down to a stone footbridge. Turn right, taking the Permissive Path, right, down to the stream. The path, uneven in places, follows the stream along the steep valley sides. Keeping to the left bank, the footpath enters the woodland of Ogden Water. After about 300 yards a junction of paths appears ahead. Take the right fork (but not across the bridge) to follow the reservoir shoreline. A path appears on the left which leads directly back to the car park. The shoreline path leads back to the Visitor Centre above the dam. If returning to Halifax by bus, an option is to take Ogden Lane from the car park to Causeway Foot on the main road, where the pub is almost opposite the bus stop which has a shelter.

14

Mytholmroyd & Cragg Vale

Distance: 4¾ miles (7½ km). Time: 3½ hours.
Terrain: main ascent of 525 feet (160m), mostly on footpaths. Some paths uneven and muddy with short steep sections.
Start and finish: Mytholmroyd railway station. Cut-off point: Cragg Vale
Transport: half hourly trains to Mytholmroyd from Leeds, Manchester Victoria, and Rochdale; hourly to Halifax, Bradford and Dewsbury. Regular buses from Halifax, Todmorden and Hebden Bridge.
Cragg Vale: hourly bus C from Hebden Bridge and Mytholmroyd.
Refreshments: Cragg Vale and Mytholmroyd. Toilets: Bridge End, Mytholmroyd.

This walk along the valley of Cragg Vale starts with a hillside route and returns along the river. Cragg Vale seems to epitomise the best of Calderdale, with little lost mill buildings, ancient stone causeways and steps up the hillsides, expanses of native woodland and fine views over the moorland tops. The area is also associated with the infamous coiners of the eighteenth century: a band of counterfeiters who cut the edges off genuine coins to create their own. Once discovered, the coiners' response was the murder of the investigating official which led to the arrest of thirty counterfeiters and execution of the leaders.

Mytholmroyd has the distinction of being the birthplace of Ted Hughes, the famous writer and poet who graphically described the moody Calderdale landscape. At Mytholmroyd station, there are boards featuring excerpts from Hughes' famous children's classic The Iron Man. *On the westbound platform, a noticeboard describes other waymarked walks that start here.*

From the station (from either platform) go down to the viaduct over the main road, and turn left. Take the next turn left on to Scout Road. Turn right up Hall Bank Lane, passing the Methodist church. Go left at the junction and then to the right of the Thomson car park, and follow the lane with the lampposts.

Go up the lane which ascends in a cutting. At the next junction take the tarmac lane on the right, over a cattle grid and then the left fork. At the cottages, go left up the cobbled track, then take an immediate right to go through the gate to follow an enclosed grassy path. Ignoring the path turning off right, continue into the wood, following the waymark posts, the path soon levelling out after dropping a few yards. After crossing a series of small streams, the path goes through a gate; take the left fork. After climbing a few yards the path passes along a walled embankment and the remains of a building. At the next waymark post, go right to descend again.

Go to the next waymark, cross over a stream, thereafter the path gets muddier and wider, and a drier path parallels it to the left. Emerging from the wood take the right fork through the gate to descend a grassy lane to the houses. Go to the front of the row of houses (Upper Birks) then turn immediately left in front of the houses, looking out for a waymark on the gate ahead. Go through the gate, then keeping to the right, over a stile and up to a farmhouse. Turn right to take a footpath which leads to a concrete track. Turn left on the concrete lane to go round the bend and up the slope, then pass the next house up to the top of the ridge.

Views over Calderdale open out towards Hebden Bridge Old Town and, to the south, towards Withens Clough Reservoir and the moors and woods above Cragg Vale.

Where the track bends left, take the path at the corner via a stile (to the left of the gate) continuing along the ridge, passing above the house with the Magnet Ale sign. At the track, turn right to take the path leading off to the left, descending to a gate with a prominent 'Shut this gate' sign. Just after the gate, take the mini-gate left, the path crossing diagonally down over the heathery field. The path levels out and rounds the edge of the woods below. At the junction of paths (GR 00372, 23264), go straight ahead, on the stone paved path which continues on the level at first, before a steady descent into the valley. At the junction turn right to carry on down to the road. Cross it and turn right to take the next left, Church Bank Lane, down to the church below. Pass the church and cross over the bridge.

Take the path which runs just to the right of the Hinchcliffe Restaurant & Bar and enter the woods, following the Cragg Brook downstream. The path climbs above the steep bank of the brook; where it splits, take the right fork to descend to the bridge.

This part of the walk follows the Cragg Brook downstream to Mytholmroyd, following its descent though waterfalls and woods and remains of old mills built into the steep wooded banks.

Go over the bridge and then take the path left which runs along the brook before rejoining the tarmac lane. Just before the lane joins the road, take the path left (small waymark on the wall) which runs along a walled terrace before descending to the next bridge. Cross the bridge and go through the gate on the right taking the footpath signed for Paper Mill Wood. Where the path forks at a gate, take the right fork to remain in the wood, following the wall as the Cragg Brook drops away below.

16

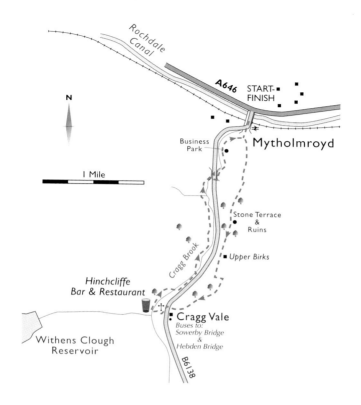

At the waymark post, bend right to descend once again towards the river, going through a waymarked gate and through a clearing. By the old bridge take the Permissive path signed to Clough Foot Bridge, the path start marked by a stile (which looks like a small seat). The path descends to the riverbank and then emerges by stables. Turn left to take the next path on the right, signed for Dauber Bridge, through a gate to follow the Cragg Brook downstream again. After crossing a tributary stream, the path leads up to a track. Turn right to continue down to Dauber Bridge and the main road.

Turn right to go up the road for about 50 yards, then take the path on the opposite side up a narrow flight of steps. Turn left at the top, following the path to the junction near the business park. Then turn left again, to follow the path round the perimeter of the business park, keeping level. The path ends at a street; follow this down to the junction and turn left to pass the Methodist Church at the start of the walk. Retrace your steps to the station by heading for the main road and turning right.

Luddenden Dean to Hebden Bridge

> **Distance: 4½ miles (7km). 5 miles (8km) to Hebden Bridge station.**
> **Time: 2½ - 3 hours.**
> **Terrain: steep slopes; 650 feet (200m) ascent, paths can be boggy. Short section crosses open moorland – navigation difficult in low cloud or fog.**
> **Start: Booth. Finish: Hebden Bridge.**
> **Transport: half hourly bus service to Booth from Halifax (not Sundays).**
> **Frequent trains and buses from Hebden Bridge to Halifax, Bradford, Leeds, Manchester Victoria and Burnley.**
> **Parking: Halifax centre – catch bus to Booth; return from Hebden Bridge.**
> **Refreshments and toilets at Hebden Bridge.**

Although the bus takes the odd diversion on its way up to Luddenden Dean, the ride is well worth it as it allows you to start the walk close to a nature reserve in a spectacular setting. The route, between two valleys, is short and steep but highly spectacular – from the intimate Luddenden Dean, with a landscape reminiscent of the Yorkshire Dales further north, over the Wadsworth Moor to Calderdale itself. The descent offers some of the best views imaginable of the famous Calderdale landmarks.

From Booth bus stop terminus, follow the road down through Booth hamlet to the river, crossing the bridge, and up as far as the sharp right bend. Here a driveway peels off left, and the footpath begins, signed 'Jerusalem Farm'. Go through the woodland passing over the bridge by the pond, past the tree stump sculptures, then take the left fork down to the river bridge.

Jerusalem Farm is a nature reserve set in beautiful woodland along the banks of the Luddenden Brook with a waterfall entrance and wood carvings made from tree stumps. The woodland is host to a wide variety of animals and plants.

Keep on the same side of the river to take the path leading upstream via a steep bank alongside the river. Take the stile by the gate and go straight ahead to the left of the posts. The path goes through some trees before dropping back down to the river to cross by a wooden bridge.

The path now goes up a slope following the left bank of a small stream,

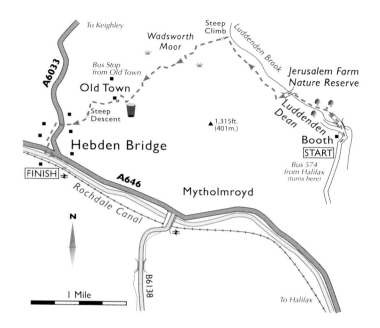

climbing past the houses; after passing the terraced garden the path reaches a lane. Turn right to take the next left fork.

Follow the track for the next ¾ mile (1km), where it descends to a turreted gatehouse flanking both sides of the track. Through the gateway go straight ahead to take the path which leads left and steeply up, the path marked by a signpost by the double gates.

Keeping to the edge of the field, the path climbs steeply up the slope onto the moor top. Cross over the path to continue in the same direction over the moor. After about 100 yards the path joins a wider path; continue in the same direction (GR 01640 28896). After about 100 yards there is another junction, turn left and after about 50 yards turn right onto another path (GR 01517 28750). This soon crosses the watershed and a view of Calderdale appears ahead.

If the conditions are right, a stunning vista of Calderdale appears and accompanies you on your descent via Old Town towards Hebden Bridge. Ahead on the right is the hilltop village of Heptonstall, while on the left the obelisk of the Peace Memorial stands on the brooding ridge of Stoodley Pike.

The path descends to an outside corner of a fence, where it also meets another fence. Turn right, and after about 20 yards, take the stile left where there is a path in a wide enclosed strip of rough pasture, narrowing as it goes down the slope. Follow this down to the lane, avoiding the section blocked by rushes near the bottom by keeping to the right side of the shallow gully.

Turn left then follow the track downhill, taking the second right (opposite the Kelham Farm sign). Follow the track down to the road. Turn right on the road.

Past the house named 'Top oth' hill', on the other side of the road take the path in front of the large stone building, which then turns right as a walled path round a whitewashed house.

Follow the path downhill, where it ends, meeting another path; go down the cobbled path to the road. Turn right to go up to Ibbotroyd. Immediately after Ibbotroyd take the waymarked path left. Follow the wall and go through a gate and stile, before turning left, taking the left fork of the two paths ahead.

The path descends steeply into a valley, and at the next junction turn left then right (before the bridge) to continue down the narrow valley.

Greater woodrush: found in a variety of habitats including wood and moorland

Follow the path down the valley until it emerges at Keighley Road. Cross the road at the traffic lights, to go down Lees Road, leading off to the right down the slope. Then go down Foster Lane, and take the first left to the bottom, then turn left again onto Victoria Road. Follow this road as it leads past the market place into Hebden Bridge town centre. From the market place, go over the bridge to the pedestrian precinct.

To reach the railway station follow the pedestrian precinct parallel to the river down to the main road. Turn left to cross the main road to go into the park (signed for railway station). Cross over the canal, and turn left after the bridge; follow the path up to the station approach road. Turn right to cross the river to get to the station.

Heptonstall & Hardcastle Crags

> **Distance: 6 miles (10 km). Time: 3 - 3½ hours.**
> **Terrain: steep ascent and descent of 720 feet (220m), mostly on footpaths.**
> **Start and finish: Hebden Bridge station/town centre**
> **Alternative start: Heptonstall. Cut-off point: Slack**
> **Transport: frequent trains to Hebden Bridge from Manchester Victoria,**
> **Rochdale, Leeds, Halifax and Bradford; hourly trains from Blackburn and**
> **Burnley, buses from Halifax, Burnley and Keighley. To Heptonstall: Bus E**
> **and 591 (2 per hour in total; Bus E also passes Slack) from Hebden Bridge**
> **railway station and town centre.**
> **Refreshments at Heptonstall, Gibson Mill (weekends only in winter),**
> **Hebden Bridge. Toilets at Hebden Bridge, Heptonstall (summer only),**
> **Gibson Mill, Hardcastle Crags.**

This walk takes in the spectacular hilltop village of Heptonstall with its superb views over Calderdale before crossing the ridge to descend into the steeply wooded Hebden Dale and Hardcastle Crags, a favourite destination of many visitors and now administered by the National Trust.

From the station go down the station drive, then turn left to go through the park following the canal. Go over the bridge through the gardens and cross the main road in the town centre by the traffic lights on the left. Turn right to go down Bridge Gate. Where the pedestrian zone starts, go over the old bridge, then take the cobbled lane leading up the hill, marked by an old sign on the wall indicating the way to Heptonstall.

At the top of the lane turn right onto the road, then past the national speed limit sign take the footpath going up on the left. At the top join the road to carry on into the centre of Heptonstall. Just before the post office, take Church Lane which leads off ahead. Passing the churchyard (the steps up lead to an information board by the churchyard), take Church Lane which winds in between old cottages before ending at a fork past the church. Take the left track, and cross the road to take the footpath signed ahead, threading between the houses.

Ahead a dramatic view of Calderdale suddenly appears with a steep drop below; looking westward one has a fine view across towards Stoodley Pike and its landmark obelisk memorial.

Turn sharp right to follow the path along the edge of the steep ridge. Once

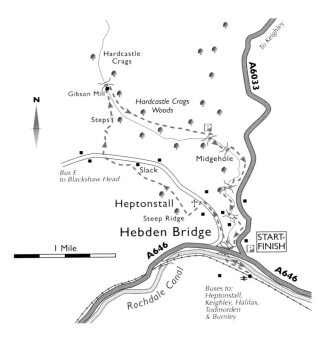

in the woodland, the path drops slightly to join another path before continuing again in the same direction. The path emerges by a tarmac lane. Turn left to descend temporarily before taking the path on the right which levels out and climbs again. At the fork, take the right path (signed 'BW Slack'). Go up the path which leads to a row of houses. Just past the houses, turn left onto a track; at the end of the row take the grassy path which follows the wall up the slope, passing two signposted paths leading off left. Past Sunny Bank (the next house) continue to the top of the common and cross the road by the 30mph signs, to take the track opposite.

After about 20 yards turn right taking the path signed for Hardcastle Crags. Then take the next path right, also signed for the crags, which leads down a walled path. Descend by the house to the road, then turn left. Take the next footpath on the right by Acre Farm through the gate, then take the stile over the fence and descend the field path straight down the slope.

Where an old wooden gate appears ahead, go through to enter the woodland below. Turn left to take the path which descends steeply by means of stone steps. At the junction, take the track ahead which descends gradually. At Gibson Mill, cross the river by the bridge to go through the mill complex.

22

Gibson Mill is a restored nineteenth century cotton mill run by the National Trust. After the Second World War it lay disused for fifty years but now houses exhibitions and events and is a showcase for sustainable development run with minimum impact on its environment. Refreshments are available but there is an admission charge. The surrounding Hardcastle Crags, renowned as a local beauty spot, is an area of woodland set in the deep valley of Hebden Dale.

The next section through the woods of Hardcastle Crags offers two options, either by means of the track, taking the upper route, or the much slower and uneven riverside path.

The track runs for about a mile through the woods of Hardcastle Crags to the main entrance and car parks. Follow the road down and turn sharp right by the bus stop to descend to the bridge. (If on the riverside path, the path emerges by the bridge.)

Cross the bridge to take the path left by the river, passing the Blue Pig pub. Take the left fork which then crosses the river and meets a lane. Turn left to go up to the road.

Gibson Mill

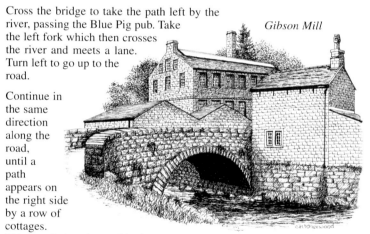

Continue in the same direction along the road, until a path appears on the right side by a row of cottages.

This runs below the road in the woodland, and just before the next house, steps appear on the right. Descend the steps and cross the drive to take the path returning to the riverside. The path passes a weir, taking a narrow course between the river on the right and a mill race on the left, before crossing the river. Now the path follows the river closely downstream, passing a cricket ground before ending by a humpbacked bridge. Cross over the bridge and follow the street along, turning right to go down the slope, and follow Victoria Road as it winds down to the market place.

If heading for the railway station, retrace your steps from the town centre or follow the directions at the end of Walk 6.

Todmorden to Hebden Bridge

Length: 5¾ miles (9.5 km). Time: 3 - 3½ hours.
Terrain: tracks, paths, some that can get boggy. An ascent of 650 feet (200m).
Parking: Todmorden town centre or Hebden Bridge town centre
Start: Todmorden Town Hall, Todmorden town centre.
Finish: Hebden Bridge railway station. Buses to Halifax and Todmorden leave from Rochdale Road.
Cut off point: Lumbutts or Mankinholes. Buses run every two hours back to Todmorden.
Public Transport: frequent trains to Todmorden from Leeds, half hourly from Bradford and Dewsbury all towards Manchester Victoria. Frequent service from Hebden Bridge back to Todmorden as well as Bradford Interchange, Dewsbury, Leeds, Manchester and Burnley.
Refreshments and toilets at Todmorden, Lumbutts (pub), Hebden Bridge.

Dominated by Stoodley Pike, this walk takes a middle level route along the hillside above Calderdale with wide views over the surrounding moors and valley below. In the hamlets of Lumbutts and Mankinholes fragments of the past are beautifully preserved in ancient farmsteads with their narrow mullioned windows, the old stone causeway and watermill. In contrast to the open expanses crossed by London Road, the dramatic descent into Hebden Bridge passes through woodland to finish by the railway station.

From Todmorden railway station go left from the station building and down the steps of White Hart Fold (signpost for Tourist Information Centre). The town hall is the large domed building by the road junction. From here, facing the road junction, take the road signed for Rochdale. Cross by the pelican lights and follow the road over the canal bridge.

Turn left at the Golden Lion pub, then take the narrow lane straight ahead, Honey Hole Road (signed for the Calderdale Way). Past the Todmorden Unitarian Church, at the junction go straight ahead up the tarmac path signed as 'Honey Hole' and up the steps. Turn left at the top, to follow the street round to meet Bank Street, then 10 yards ahead go up the steps on the right.

Take the next flight of steps up to the street and continue up the next steps over the road in between the modern houses.

Go left past a pillar box, crossing Longfield Way and up the steps. At the top take the track ahead which runs behind Longfield Terrace.

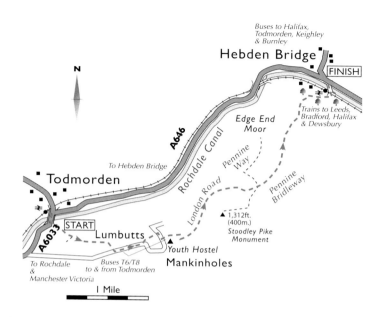

The track climbs steadily; take the left fork and past the houses and yard, bend right on the track and then take the footpath on the left, just before an old cattle grid. The path takes a direction roughly at 10 o'clock across the field to an old gateway (marked by prominent stones) just to the right of a telegraph pole. Next head for the stile straight ahead and the path now follows a drystone wall up a gentle slope. At the top the path descends with the wall on the right to an enclosed lane.

Turn right to follow the lane past some houses down to a road, Lumbutts Lane. Turn left to continue along the road down the slope into Lumbutts, keeping straight ahead at the 30mph signs. Cross the bridge and take the path leading up on the left, signed as the Pennine Bridleway.

Over the bridge the remains of Lumbutts Mill stand over the river, some of the mill complex now converted into housing.

Passing Top Brink Inn, the bridleway continues to the left of the inn buildings and takes the form of an enclosed stone causeway which winds its way towards Mankinholes. Follow the Pennine Bridleway sign into the hamlet.

Just before the youth hostel, turn left on the track. Follow this until the next junction, then turn left up to the twin gate. Turn left onto the track, known as London Road. The route along this section is a long stretch on the track running right under Stoodley Pike and the landmark memorial.

The Stoodley Pike memorial was built to commemorate the end of the Crimean war in 1854, replacing an earlier memorial (for the end of the war with Napoleon in 1814) which had collapsed when damaged by lightning.

At the highest point reached by the track, the Pennine Way crosses; shortly before Swillington Farm, continue straight ahead through the gate along the track. Follow the track to the cross roads, keeping straight ahead as the Pennine Bridleway turns off. The track passes a cluster of houses under a hill slope, before emerging at a cross roads, marked by a 'No Motor Vehicles' sign on the right.

Take the track straight ahead through a gate, shortly after bending left to go downhill.

On the way down allotments appear on the left, a testament to the ingenuity of local growers able to cultivate the wet poor soils of the Pennines, 900 feet (275m) above sea level.

At the path junction, go straight ahead, to descend further under a bridge to the wood, then keep left to continue the descent. At the junction turn right to continue downhill, going all the way in the same direction, ignoring turn offs, directly to the bottom of the hill to meet a concrete track. Turn left to take the concrete track under the railway bridge and take the next left to emerge by Hebden Bridge railway station.

Stoodley Pike

26

Todmorden & Redmires Water

Length: 6 miles (9.5km). Time: 3½ - 4 hours.
Terrain: paths, some steep sections. Ascents total 820 feet (250m).
Start & Finish: Todmorden railway station.
Transport: frequent trains from Leeds, Halifax, Manchester Victoria,
Rochdale and Bradford, hourly from Burnley and Dewsbury. Buses from
Halifax, Rochdale, Burnley and Rossendale.
Parking: Todmorden town centre
Cut off point: Burnley Road, half hourly buses serving Todmorden,
Halifax, Hebden Bridge and Burnley.
Refreshments/facilities: plenty in Todmorden – toilets at Brook Street.

The upper reaches of Calderdale lie in a steep gorge that culminates in a narrow gap forced through the gritstone hills by glacial action – the route used by the road and railway to Burnley in Lancashire. The walk climbs steadily out of Todmorden to take an elevated route above this upper part of Calderdale along the edges of the moors. The steep eroded sides of the valley are symptomatic of the vulnerability of this area to severe flooding. After a descent through the dramatic gorge of Redmires Water, the return is on the opposite side of the valley at a lower level, passing above the Centre Vale Park on a cycle route which leads directly to the station and town centre.

From the station go round the station approach road and under the railway viaduct, then after 20 yards take the lower path, right, to go behind the college. Go down the steps, right, to pass the college, and cross the main road. Go to Wellington Road, just to the right of the row of shops. Follow Wellington Road past the rows of terraced houses, up the hill to the dead end. Then take the footbridge over the railway, and the path up to the road.

Turn right and then take the left turn at the next bend, on the track signed up to The Hollins. Turn left at the Hollins, taking the path down through the gap to another street end. Follow this down and over the bridge to the crossroads. Take the path straight ahead, along the passageway; the path crosses a steep gully before going through the trees up to a concrete drive which leads behind a house. At the junction turn right up another concrete drive leading up to farm buildings. Turn left and take the path leading through a narrow gap and gate through the field to the next gap. The path follows the wall into the woods, before bending left to drop to a street.

Now turn right and take the short street spur that leads off on the right and the footpath that leads off from the end. The grassy path is a steep climb up, well waymarked at first.

A triple waymark appears, take the path going straight ahead, it becoming less distinct further up the slope, passing to the left of a pond, then head at a direction of 11 o' clock up the slope to meet a track near the boundary fence. Go up and through the gate to take the enclosed path up towards the farm (can be boggy after wet weather).

Go up past the farm, taking the track leading up the slope to the junction, and turn left. Follow this track up to the gate, and continue straight ahead, the surface becoming a stone causeway.

The path passes below the craggy summit of Great Bride Stones Moor and the boulder field of Whirlaw Stones.

At the next gate, the path is joined by the Todmorden Centenary Way; continue in the same direction, the path becoming an enclosed lane. After about 375 yards, the Calderdale Way branches off left. Continue on the upper track, for another ¾ mile (1.2km), passing a plantation and dipping into a shallow valley before meeting a crossroads of tracks with a signpost for each direction.

Turn left to go down an enclosed lane to the next junction. Turn left here onto the track to go to Hartley Royd. Go past the old house through the courtyard, with a plantation wood on your right. Where the track enters a field, take the path which runs to the left of the track to the radio mast. Follow this wide green path as it runs above Redmires Water, gradually descending. Keep to the track as it takes its winding, gentle descent.

At this point the path gives a grand view over the precipitous gorge of Redmires Water, a truly dramatic location, hidden away from the main Calder Valley.

At the next junction of paths, turn left to take the path through the clearing, then entering a wood. The path then meets a track, which is the end of a street, Knotts Road. Follow the road down past the houses, and over the little bridge over the railway to meet Burnley Road.

Tormentil

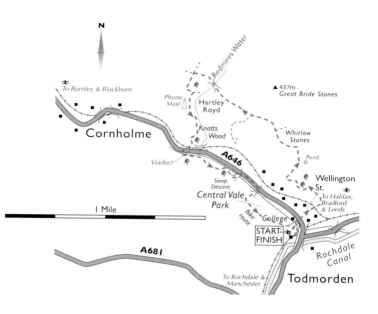

Turn left, and after the bend cross the road with care to take the track leading from the opposite side, crossing the river. Take the track leading off to the left. This forks by a house; take the right fork. This wide path climbs up to a stile. Go over the stile and then take the left lower path which leads ahead, climbing only slightly. After passing under a tree, the path reaches another junction. Turn left to go down the hill through the woodland.

At the base of the slope, take the track left to go back down to Burnley Road. Turn right, and follow the road past the hotel entrance and the school. Just at the main school entrance, turn right to take the signed footpath and cycle route to Todmorden Town Centre (1 mile/1.5km). The cycleway starts at the back of the sports centre car park, running along the edge of the parkland. After entering the woodland the path splits; you can follow the tarmac cycle path or take the path which forks to the left, but maintain your height to rejoin eventually the tarmac cycle path further on.

The path continues until it emerges at Well Lane. Take the Ridge steps leading down from Well Lane, then turn right at the bottom. Follow the road round under the viaduct, to meet the Station Approach road again.

Walsden & Gorpley Reservoir

Distance: 5¾ miles (9.2km). Time: 3½ - 4 hours.
Terrain: footpaths, some boggy on exposed tops. Ascent of 980 feet (300m).
Start: Walsden railway station. Finish: Todmorden railway station.
Transport: hourly trains to Walsden from Halifax, Bradford, Leeds,
Manchester and Rochdale. Buses from Todmorden and Rochdale. Frequent
trains to Todmorden from Halifax, Bradford and Leeds, Manchester and
Rochdale. Buses to Halifax, Burnley and Rossendale.
Parking: Todmorden town centre. No public car park in Walsden.
Refreshments: pub, chip shop in Walsden; cafes, pubs and toilet in Todmorden.

At its westernmost point, this walk runs along the Lancashire border on the watershed of the rivers Calder and Irwell (and so effectively the watershed of the North and Irish Seas). Though short, this is the highest of our ten walks and passes through some demanding terrain where navigation is difficult under low cloud or misty conditions. The final part goes through field paths and woods before descending into Todmorden with a direct path to the railway station and town centre.

Walsden lies in a tributary valley of the Calder, forced through by a glacier and forming an effective gap in the Pennines albeit rather narrow. Walsden itself has had a long history of settlement, with stone age flints found in Ramsden Clough and Trough End nearby. Many farms date from the fifteenth century. The name Walsden derives from the Old English meaning 'valley of the Welshmen'. In the 1850s there was a boom in cotton mills, powered first by local streams and then coal.

From the station, if travelling by bus or by train from Yorkshire, cross the railway tracks using the footbridge to Clough Road. Otherwise take the platform exit onto Clough Road from the eastbound platform. Then turn right onto Kershaw Road. Go up the hill passing the rows of terraced houses and at the end of the street take the wider of the two paths, leading off left.

Follow the path up through the woods to the top boundary wall. Turn left onto the path, then the next right – the footpath signs are on a post by a gate. Follow the fence up the gentle slope, and go to the left of the house. At the top of the drive, go over the stile to take the path leading straight ahead up the slope via a series of stiles. The path ends at a corner of a field. Go over the stile and turn right onto the track. Cross over the cattle grid, then take the second track right, to bypass the farm.

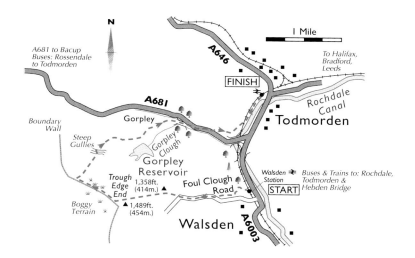

Under the power lines, take the footpath that leads off right, then veers off left by the first mast to ascend the hill steadily. Head up the hill towards the twin wall and fence ahead. A stile takes the path up the right side of the fence and wall. Ascending the top, the path levels and there is a gradual and slight descent before the final climb to the hilltop of Trough Edge End.

As you climb up fine views of Calderdale open up behind. At the top, you can look all the way down towards Rochdale, Oldham and Manchester. Further along the ridge the valley of Rossendale can be seen.

At the summit a triangulation point appears. Turn left to go through the gate, and then turn immediately right, keeping to the left of the pond, to follow the fence and wall again, heading for the yellow waymark post on a stile ahead.

Climb over the stile to head along the wall, which now forms the boundary with Lancashire. Follow the wall along the ridge top, passing a footpath sign for Limers Gate on the way. Head for the tall ladder-stile (on the boundary wall) ahead.

Limers Gate is the name of an old route that linked the limestone quarries of Clitheroe with Rochdale. Lime was in demand as it reduced the acidity of the poor land underlain by gritstone.

At the tall ladder-stile, turn right to head for a marker post for the footpath leading downhill. After the first post, continue in the same direction (ignoring the posts leading off to the left), to follow the posts leading down past the old coalmines (which used to feed the mill engines in Walsden) on the right, to a track, with a signpost for Gorpley Reservoir.

Head straight down in the direction of the sign, towards the drystone wall surrounding the green fields below. At first, the path follows to the left of a shallow gully, and then passes a shaft marked by several wooden posts, descending through tussock grass.

As you approach the stone wall, yellow waymarked posts come into view by the wall. The footpath crosses two gullies, the second considerably steeper. The path then follows the wall round to a prominent stile and then parallels the wall to where a track begins. Keeping to the left of the wall, the track winds round and, after a gate, goes steeply down the hill. Approaching the white house, the track bends left. Go through the electrically operated gates – the open and close buttons are on the right-hand-side post. Join the tarmac lane at the bend and go straight ahead.

Go through the gate at Gorpley Cottage then down in front of the house (Gorpley Farm). Turn left to go through the gate, then right to follow the fence down the hill, over the stile, then left down the end of Gorpley Clough.

The path winds down through the wood to descend to the road, bending right by the iron-stained stream to reach a small car park bay. Turn right onto the road, and just past the house cross the road to take the footpath left, which leads up the slope.

Going through the woods, the path then levels out as it crosses a field, and at the junction of paths by a ruined barn, turn left for a short ascent before levelling off again; bend right. Head for the gap-stile in the right-hand corner of the walls. Go past the stables, going straight ahead in front of the farm. At the far end of the drive, go over the stile and turn left.

A surprise view of the main valley dropping sharply below is suddenly before you; immediately below are the trans-Pennine routes all squeezed in the valley floor – canal, railway and road.

Cross the walled path down to the tarmac lane below, meeting it at the apex of a bend. Turn right to continue your descent. At Stones Road Junction, go straight ahead down the dead-end lane. Continue downhill to the level crossing over the railway and cross with care. Then turn left to follow the joint cycleway and footpath directly to Todmorden station.